English Grammar & Composition at the Primary Level, including Unseen Passages

A Common Guidebook for Standards 1, 2, 3 & 4

P. Sarkar

(With an Attempt to Cover Syllabi of CBSE, ICSE, NIOS, CISCE, and Other School Boards as the Common Guidebook for All.)

First Edition- October 2024

Last Updated: 24-10-2024

Made with ❤ on the Amazon & Notion Press Platform.

https://kdp.amazon.com/en_US/ & https://notionpress.com/

DEDICATION

This book is lovingly dedicated to all the wonderful little kids in classes 1 to 4.

BOOK SUMMARY

In the current project focused on grammar books for various classes, Mr. Sarkar has made a concerted effort to simplify English grammar and writing skills for primary-level students. He conducted extensive research on the syllabi of different state and national school boards to identify a common thread. While some boards emphasize specific chapters of English grammar, others overlook them entirely. Mr. Sarkar has aimed to synthesize these varying approaches and present them as a cohesive English grammar and composition summary.

As a result, his book may not fully align with any single syllabus from boards in the country or abroad. Still, he believes it will give students a holistic understanding of English grammar and Composition, enabling them to grasp the subject more effectively and write composition more fluently.

Regarding composition, Mr. Sarkar has primarily relied on everyday language and selected familiar topics to engage his loving young readers.

Thanking you
Author (s)

CONTENTS

Contents **Pages**

ACKNOWLEDGMENTS

In the current project involving grammar books for various classes, Mr. Sarkar collaborates with Mr. Peter. He expresses his gratitude to the boards of CBSE, ICSE, and various State School Boards of India for providing curricula on their respective websites.

Throughout his research, Mr. Sarkar identified what would benefit young children and incorporated those insights into his books for different grade levels. For the primary English Grammar and Writing Skills, Mr. Sarkar relies heavily on Mr. Peter's works and CBSE and ICSE demonstration methods.

Additionally, for illustrations, images, and scientific information, Mr. Sarkar is indebted to various sources, including Encyclopedia Britannica, en.wikipedia.org, solarsystem.nasa.gov, freely available images from Bing and Microsoft Stock Images, and depends on various AI tools like ChatGPT, Sider, Grammarly, and Playground.

1. Alphabet (*A* to *Z*)

(1) Fill in the blanks:

A for ______________________

B for ______________________

C for ______________________

D for ______________________

E for ______________________

F for ______________________

G for ______________________

H for ______________________

I for ______________________

J for ______________________

K for ______________________

L for ______________________

M for ______________________

N for ______________________

O for ______________________

P for ______________________

Q **for** ______________________	
R **for** ______________________	
S **for** ______________________	
T **for** ______________________	
U **for** ______________________	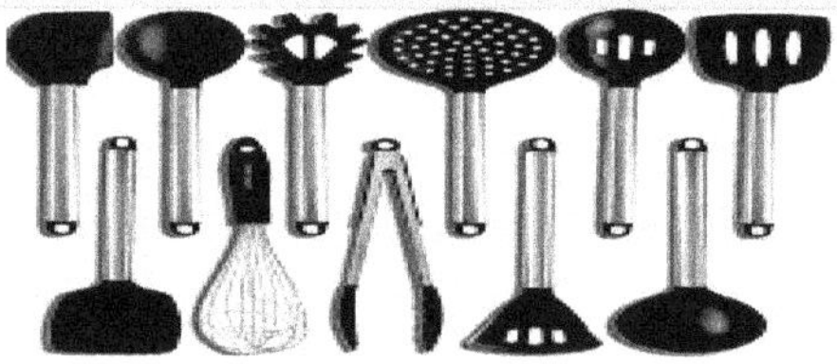
V **for** ______________________	
W **for** ______________________	
X **for** ______________________	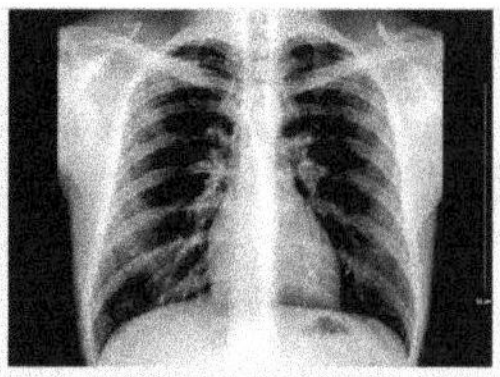
Y **for** ______________________	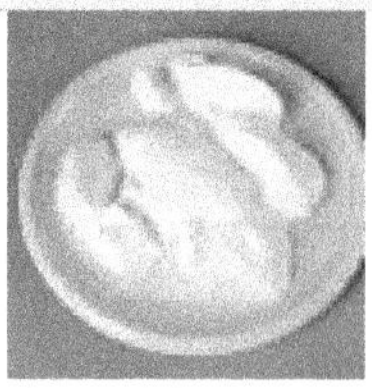

Z for ____________________

Check your answer:

A. Ant = Ants are eusocial insects of the family Formicidae and belong to the order Hymenoptera, along with the related wasps and bees.

B. Butterfly = Butterflies, including moths, are insects in the macro lepidopteran clade Rhopalocera from the order Lepidoptera. Adult butterflies have large, often brightly colored wings and conspicuous, fluttering flight.

C. Carrot = The carrot is a root vegetable, typically orange in color, though purple, black, red, white, and yellow cultivars exist. All of these are domesticated forms of the wild carrot, which is eatable both raw and cooked.

D. Dolphin = A dolphin is an aquatic mammal within the infra-order Cetacea. There are 40 extant species named as dolphins in our world.

E. Eggplant = **Eggplant** or brinjal, mainly used in cooking as vegetable food

F. Frog = A frog is any member of a diverse and primarily carnivorous group of short-bodied, tailless amphibians.

G. Gift-box = a box containing gifts,

H. The hippo or Hippopotamus (large hippo) is a large semiaquatic mammal native to sub-Saharan Africa. The other is the pygmy hippopotamus. Its name comes from the ancient Greek for "river horse."

I. **Island =** any area of land smaller than a continent and entirely surrounded by water. **Islands** may occur in oceans, seas, lakes, or rivers.

J. Jug = a type of container, used to hold liquids.

K. Keyboard = an input device of a computer

L. Leaf = plural form ‘leaves. Leaf is the kitchen of plants and trees where plants produce its food in the presence of sunlight.

M. Moon = The Moon is Earth's only natural satellite. It revolves round our earth in about 29 and half days (29 d 12 h 44 min 2.9 s).

N. Nightingale = The common nightingale bird is a small passerine bird, best known for its powerful and beautiful song. It was formerly classed as a member of the thrush family.

O. Owl = Owls are night prey birds with over 200 species, mostly live in solitary places or in the trunk of trees during days.

P. Panda = The giant panda, also known as the panda bear, is a bear species endemic to China. It is characterized by its bold black-and-white coat and rotund body. There is another species, red panda.

Q. Quail = A common quail bird is a small ground-nesting game bird. It is a migratory bird that is also seen in Africa and southern India. With its characteristic call of three repeated chirps, a quail is more often heard than seen.

R. Raccoon = The raccoon is a mammal, unlike monkeys, a carnivore animal found in forests.

S. Star = A star is **an astronomical object.** Our Sun is also a star. Many other stars are visible to the naked eye at night.

T. Tiger = The tiger is the largest living cat species and a member of the genus Panthera.

U. Utensils = a tool, container, or other article, especially for household use.

V. Vase = A **vase** is an open container. It can be made from several materials, such as ceramics, glass, and non-rusting metals, such as aluminum, brass, bronze, etc.

W. Wolf = **Wolves** are large, four-legged, carnivorous mammals. They hunt together, found in forests.

X. x-ray = An X-ray is a quick, painless test that produces images of the structures inside your body — mainly your bones.

Y. Yogurt = **Yogurt** is a popular dairy product made by the bacterial fermentation of milk.

Z. Zucchini = The **zucchini** courgetti or baby marrow (Cucurbita pepo) is a summer squash.

(2) Write more than one word: (minimum 3, and maximum 7)

For examples:

***A* for** Avocado, arm, ambulance, astronaut, airplane, alligator, axe.

***B* for** ____

***C* for** ____

***D* for** ____

***E* for** ____

***F* for** ____

***G* for** ____

***H* for**____

***I* for** ____

***J* for** ____

K **for** ____

L **for** ____

M **for**____

N **for** ____

O **for** ____

P **for** ____

Q **for** ____

R **for** ____

S **for** ____

T **for** ____

***U* for** ____

***V* for** ____

***W* for** ______________________________________

***X* for** ____

***Y* for** ____

***Z* for** ____

Answer guide:

A. A *for* > Avocado, arm, ambulance, astronaut, airplane, alligator, axe.

B. B *for* > bird, ball, bee, balloon, banana, butterfly, bun

C. C *for* > cat, candles, cake, carrot, cherry, cupboard, carom, coin

D. D *for* > *dog, drum, dolphin, dad (father), door, dusk, dustbin, duster*

E. E *for* > egg, elephant, envelope, eggplant (brinjal), eagle,

F. F *for* > flower, fish, fence, frog, frock, football, falcon

G. G *for* > grapes, guitar, gift box, goat, gate, guineapig

H. H *for* > hat, house, hippo, hammer, hen, husband, hot-pot, hanger, house-coat

I. I *for* > ice, island, ink, inkpot, ice cream, igloo, inkjet, injection.

J. J *for* > jug, jackal, jelly, jellyfish, jelly beans, jacket, joker

K. K *for* > kite, kettle, knife, keyboard, Kolkata, Kartik

L. L *for* > leaf, lamb, lion, ladybug, lantern, lamppost,

M. M *for* > mother, mango, moon, magnet, mushroom, mermaid,

N. N *for* > nest, number, notes, net, necklace, nightingale, nurse

O. O *for* > owl, ox, orange, onion, octopus, Olivia, Olympic,

P. P *for* > paintbrush, pear, pumpkin, pig, panda, pencil, palette, pizza, penguin

Q. Q *for* > queen, quilt, quetzal, question, quince, quail

R. R *for* > rocket, rainbow, radish, roses, rain-coat, rabbit, rat, raccoon, road

S. S *for* > Sun, sandals, star, shirt, snowman, sister, ship

T. T *for* > tree, train, target, tiger, Tata, toe, Tokyo,

U. U *for* > umbrella, utensils, U-turn, UFO, unicorn, University, union,

V. V *for* > vase, vulture, van, vine, violet, violin,

W. W *for* > water, window, watermelon, wolf, watch,

X. X *for* > x-mas, xylophone, x-ray,

Y. Y *for* > yoyo, yacht, yak, yellow, yogurt, yam, yarn,

Z. Z *for* > zero, zigzag, zipper, zebra, zucchini,

(3) **Which are called the alphabet?**

- The set of letters you read, from A to Z / a to z, is called the alphabet.
- There are 26 letters in English, which are written in two methods.
- The letters (A to Z) in the first method are capital letters.

- The letters (a to z) in the second method are small letters.
- Names of people, places, and days of the week start with capital letters.
- The first letter of every sentence is always a capital letter.

Capital Letters

A	B	C	D	E	F	G	H	I
J	K	L	M	N	O	P	Q	R
S	T	U	V	W	X	Y	Z	

Small Letters

a	b	c	d	e	f	g	h	i
j	k	l	m	n	o	p	q	r
s	t	u	v	w	x	y	z	

(4) Exercise

A. Capitalize the first letter of each sentence and rewrite them.

1. we saw a bluebird. = ______________________
2. the kite flew in the sky. = ______________________
3. his name is Harish. = ______________________
4. she likes apples. = ______________________
5. my mother is pretty. = ______________________

B. Rewrite each sentence by capitalizing the required letter.

1. her aunt is coming for christmas.

   ____

2. these cherries are from himachal pradesh.

   ____

3. rohit has a new pencil box.

   ____

4. i will be a cowboy for halloween.

   ____

5. his sister is going to europe.

____

2. Arrange Words in Alphabetical Order

(5) **What is called Alphabetical order?**

- When words are arranged according to the alphabet, it is called alphabetical order.
- Alphabetical order is a way to sort a list. It makes finding a name or title in a list easier.

Example: Arrange the pictures in alphabetical order.

- Here, words are organized by their first letter. First comes A, then comes B, then comes C, and so on.
- If all the words start with the same letter, then the following letter is to be considered and thus go on.

Read another Example where the first letter of all words is the same:

- The alphabetical order for *bet, bat, boat* would be ***bat, bet, boat.***
- The alphabetical order for ***caps, candles,*** and ***cake*** would be ***cake, candles***, and ***caps.***

(6) **Exercises.** Read the picture story.

Today is Maria's birthday. Maria's mother prepared a list of things required for her birthday party.

"Happy Birthday! Maria. Let's make a list of things for your birthday party. We need **cake, candles, ice cream, caps**..." says Mumma. "**And balloons** and **gifts,** too," adds Maria.

"Let me pen down the list of all the things," says Mumma.

A. Will you now help Maria and her Mumma make a list of things in alphabetical order?
Alphabetically, the names of the articles will be thus,

____.

B. Answer the following questions.

1. Write the three things that start with the letter **C** alphabetically from the story above. ____

2. Write at least five names of your friends you would like to invite to your birthday party. Write the names in alphabetical order.

   ____

3. From the list of Maria's mother, name the thing that would be at number three when arranged alphabetically by Maria's mother.

   ____

(7) **Directions: Read each pair of words. Write the word which would come first in**

alphabetical order.

Example: lost & found

Answer: found & lost

1. Run, walk – ______________________
2. Play, sit – ______________________
3. Fast, slow – ______________________
4. Happy, smile – ______________________
5. Face, arm – ______________________
6. Look, swim – ______________
7. Jump, jog – ______________
8. Type, water – ______________
9. Friend, family – ______________
10. Stand, still – ______________

C. Read the words in each row. Then, arrange them in alphabetical order:

1) Need, plane, cute, cactus, truck, chase.

= ______________________________________

2) Plant, jeep, turtle, ship, cats, earth

= ______________________________________

3) Car, grow, little, train, mice, respect

= ______________________________________

3. Vowels and Consonants

(8) **Study the following sentences:**

- Letters that can be spoken alone are called vowels.
- Letters which cannot be spoken alone are called consonants.
- The letters **A, E, I, O, and U** are called vowels.
- The letters **B, C, D, F, G, H, J, K, L, M, N, P, Q, R, S, T, V, W, X, Y, and Z** are called consonants.

(9) **Exercises:** A balloon seller came into the colony, and he gave each child a balloon of a different color.

Now, read the picture story.

A balloon seller comes to the colony.

He gives a red balloon to Arun and a yellow balloon to Mita.

"Where is mine?" asks Raju.

A. Answer the following questions from the story given above.

1. Who comes to the colony? ______________________
2. Which balloon does the balloon seller give to Mita?

____

3. Who gets the blue balloon? ______________________

B. Underline the words that begin with vowels and circle the words that begin with consonants:

balloon, ear, yellow, red, elephant, blue, orange, inkjet, airplane, seller

(10) **Add vowels to the following letters to correctly spell an animal's name. Write the name of the animal in the blanks. The first one has been done for you.**

1. Ms = Mouse
2. Brd = ____________
3. Lmb = ____________
4. Hrs = ____________
5. Snk = ____________
6. Tgr = ____________
7. Rbbt = ____________

(11) **Colour the candy red if it has a vowel in it. Yellow if it has a consonant in it.**

(12) **Fill in the blanks with the missing vowels and consonants.**

4. Naming Words or Nouns

(13) **Everything around us has names, such as** Mita, Sita, cat, dog, bird, tree, plant, chair, table, Balurghat, the Gita, the Ganga, etc.

→ The words that we use to name people, places, animals, and things are called naming words. All the above, written in color, are examples of **Naming words.**

→ Names can be **common** and **special.**
→ Common names are names of general people, places, or things in one group or class, such as cats, dogs, birds, trees, plants, chairs, tables, etc.
→ Special names are names of specific persons, places, or things, such as Mita, Sita, Balurghat, the Gita, the Ganga, etc.

→ **Special names always begin with capital letters, such** as the Bible, The Ganga, The Gita, etc.
→ However, the special name of a person, place, or God—does not take the article 'the' before them. These are exceptions, such as Mita, Sita, Balurghat, London, etc.

→ **A name can be for one thing or person or more than one,** such as Ravi, fleet, army, police, thief, etc.

→ We can change one into many by adding the letter **'s'/ 'es'/ 'ies'** to the words, such as dog—dog, house—houses, cherry—cherries, etc.

→ The naming words that we use for boys are called **He names.**
Examples: Boy, Man, King, Nephew, and Uncle.

→ The naming words that we use for girls are called **She names.**
Examples: Girl, Woman, Queen, Niece, and Aunt, etc.

(14) **Exercises: Circle the naming words in the sentences given below. Among the names, write P for a person, PL for a place, T for a thing, and ANM for an animal.**

a) Anita is reading a book at her home. =.......
b) There are many books on the table. =.......
c) Anita's grandmother is in the kitchen. =.......
d) The clock shows the time of 19 minutes to twelve. =.......

(15) **Read the naming words in the following box and write them in the correct column.**

Dog	Teacher	Computer	Restaurant
Hospital	Nurse	Pencil	Cow
Police Station	Father	Ladybug	Eyeglasses
Chicken	Barber	Toothbrush	America

Person	**Place**	**Animal**	**Thing**
....	....	....	....
....	....	....	....
....	....	....	....
....	....	....	....

....

....

(16) **Write whether the following naming words are common or special.**

1. Mohan Sharma ______________________
2. carpenter ______________________
3. dog ______________________
4. Raju ______________________
5. book ______________________
6. subway library ______________________
7. Jupiter ______________________
8. planet ______________________
9. restaurant ______________________
10. Burger King ______________________

(17) **Add 's' or 'es' to these stars to make each word more than one.**

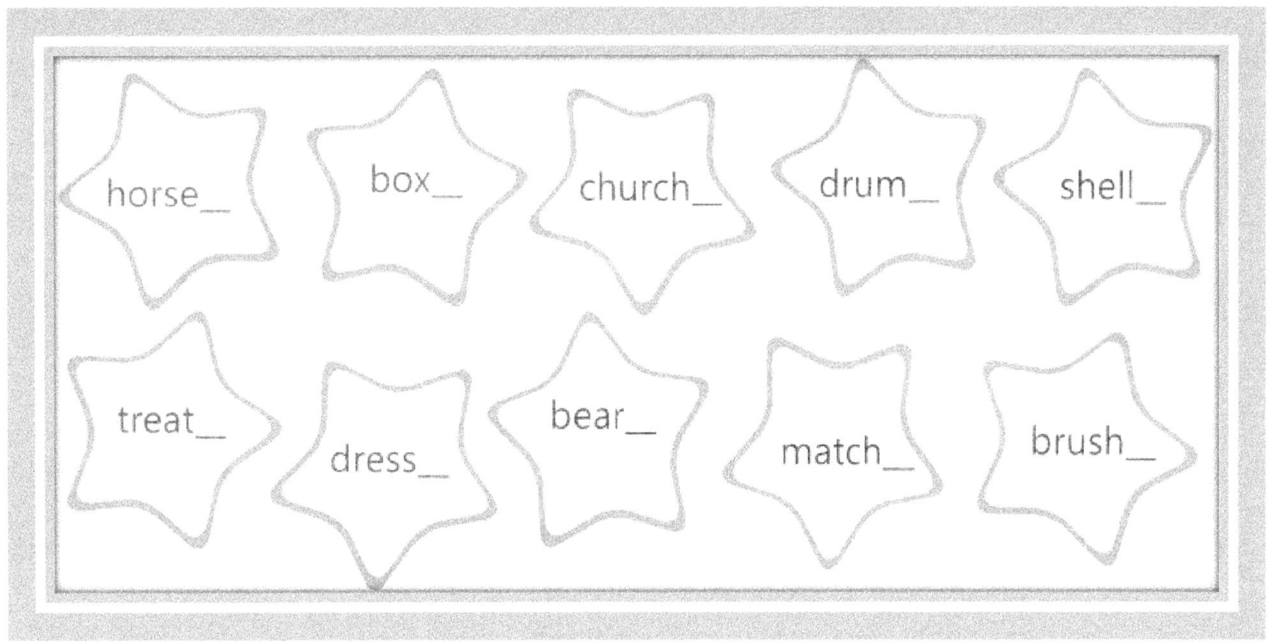

5. The Pronouns 'He,' 'She,' 'It,' and 'Me, You, & Them'

(18) **When they are used:**

Me, us, you, him, her, it, and them are also **part of other names** (or **pronouns**) that are used in place of ***I, we, you, he, she, it, they***—when used after doing words.

- **'Me'** is used in place of **'I'** when used after the verb in the sentence.
- **'Us'** is used instead of **'we'** when used after the verb in the sentence.
- **'Him'** is used in place of **'he'** when used after the verb in the sentence.
- **'Her'** is used instead of **'she'** when used after the verb in the sentence.
- **'It'** is used in place of **'an object'** or **'an animal'** when used after the verb in the sentence.
- **'Them'** is used instead of **'they'** when used after the verb in the sentence.

(19) **In the following, study through the picture story:**

I am Vikram. Call **me** Vicky.

We are students. Tell **us** a story.

She is my sister. I love **her** very much.

He is my brother. I love **him** very much.

You are my student. I tell **you** stories.

They are our parents. We love **them** dearly.

It is a pencil. Sharpen **it**, please.

They are our cows. We give **them** good grass.

You are my friend. Let me give **you** a pen.

It is a cat. Give **it** some milk.

(20) **Read the following story and answer the questions:**

"Hi Anjan, can you come to my house to play with me? We can play chess, ludo, and other games," asks Sanjukta.

"My Mother wants me to do my homework. She will let me play only after I finish it," replies Anjan.

"Fine... I will play with my dog till you come. It can run and catch my ball. You can join us after you finish your homework." says Sanjukta.

A. Answer the following questions.

1. What does Sanjukta ask Anjan?

____

2. Why does Anjan's mother not allow her to play?

____

3. Which naming word is used in place of dog?

____

B. From the story above, write naming words for the following pronouns or other names.

a. We ____________________
b. She ____________________
c. It ____________________
d. Us ____________________

(21) **Fill in the blanks with a suitable pronoun (the words used in place of Nouns).** You may choose from the list given in the box:

(Him, Her, It, They, He, She, them):

1. **Mr. Rohit** is a policeman. ____________________catches thieves.
2. **Ms. Reena** is a teacher. ____________________ teaches in a school.
3. **Boys and girls** go to school. ____________________ learn to read and write.
4. **The elephant** is a wild animal. ____________________ lives in a jungle.
5. I have **a piece of meat.** I will give ____________________ to the dog.
6. **My father** loves me, and I love ____________________ too.
7. I have **many books.** I keep ____________________ in my bag.
8. **My mother** is very lovely. I love ____________________ a lot.

(22) **Here are two sets of pronoun forms. One set is used before doing words and another after doing words or verbs. Draw a line to join each one with the other, used in place of.**

I	he	it	she	they	you	we
Us	her	you	them	me	him	it

(23) **Fill in the blanks with correct pronouns instead of the bold words. Pronouns you may choose from the above.**

1. **Pawan and I** are brothers. __________ share a bedroom.
2. **Suman** isn't well. Dad is taking __________ to see a doctor.
3. **My brother** is a teacher. __________ teaches English.
4. All **his** students like __________ very much.
5. **Children** __________ are making noise will be punished? (use either **'who,' 'whose,'** or **'whom'**)
6. Who are those **people**? Where are __________ from?
7. **Mom** is a doctor. __________ works in a hospital.
8. The sky is getting dark. __________ is going to rain.

(24) **In the pair of sentences below, one sentence is correct with the correct form of pronouns. Choose which one is correct. Write the letter 'a' or 'b' on the line to indicate the correct sentence.**

1. a) It belongs to you. – b) It belongs to your. ____________
2. a) I see his kite. – b) I see he kite. ____________
3. a) Come with us. – b) Come with we. ____________
4. a) Watch I do it – b) Watch me do it. ____________
5. a) Give it to she. – b) Give it to her. ____________
6. a) I know him best. – b) I know he best. ____________
7. a) You can have it. – b) Your can have it. ____________
8. a) It is for they. – b) It is for them. ____________
9. a) Here we come. – b) Here us come. ____________
10. a) Tell she to hurry. – b) Tell her to hurry. ____________
11. a) Give I the cat. – b) Give me the cat ____________
12. a) It is mine coat. – b) It is my coat ____________

6. Know of *'He' names* & *'She' names* (Gender)

(25) Here are some names of relations you know about in your surroundings. Some denote **'He' names,** and some denote **'She' names.** Study the table where relations are shown in two columns:

'She' names	*'He' names*
Mother	Father
Sister	Brother
Aunt	Uncle
Grandmother	Grandfather
Nieces	niece

(26) Like the above table, now you complete the following chart with names of the relation of the members at your school and some relations you know in your locality:

Column A	*Column B*
....	Principal Sir
Sister	....
....	Headmaster
Matron	....

(27) **Tick the correct option of Pronouns against the bold words on the left.**

		Tick at the right box.			*Tick at the right box.*
	He			He	
Peter is planning his project.	She		**Gita** is reading a book.	She	
		Tick at the right box			*Tick at the right box*
	He			He	
The **old man** is walking with a stick.	She		My **mother** is a renowned singer.	She	

(28) **Write now 5 'He' names looking around you that denote male names.**

1. ______________________
2. ______________________
3. ______________________
4. ______________________
5. ______________________

(29) **Write here 5 'She' names looking around you that denote female names.**

1. ______________________
2. ______________________
3. ______________________
4. ______________________
5. ______________________

(30) Can't you also name some animals you see and know from your surroundings? Try these to give their 'He' names:

'She' names	*'He' names*
Bitch	....
Cow	....
Cock-sparrow	....
Hen	....
Duck	....
Mare	....
Nun	....
Deer	....
Lamb	....
Vixen	....
Pea-hen	....
Cow-elephant	....
She-goat	....

7. Naming words; as, *One* or *More* (Numbers)

(31) **Look around your classroom and answer these questions:**

1) How many girls are there in the classroom?
2) How many boys are there in the classroom?
3) How many windows has your classroom?
4) How many doors has your classroom?
5) How many teachers are there in your school?
6) How many teacher is right now in your classroom?

(32) **Can't we say:**

Table-1

Singular Number that tells us of 'One'	*Plural Number that tells us of 'More than One'*
One **girl**	Two **girl*s***
One **boy**	Three **boy*s***
One **window**	Four **window*s***
One **door**	Five **door*s***

One **teacher**	Ten **teacher*s***

(33) Sometimes these plural forms of naming words are formed adding **'-es'** or **'-ies'** or **'-ves'** or **'changing letters'** within the naming words or Nouns.

Table-2

Singular Number that tells us of 'One'	*Plural Number that tells us of 'More than One'*
One **box**	Two **box*es***
One **dish**	Three **dish*es***
One **bus**	Four **bus*es***
One **gas**	Five **gas*es***
One **brush**	Six **brush*es***
One **class**	Seven **class*es***
One **bench**	Ten **bench*es***

Table-3

Singular Number that tells us of 'One'	*Plural Number that tells us of 'More than One'*
One **girl**	Two **girl*s***
One **boy**	Three **boy*s***
One **window**	Four **window*s***
One **door**	Five **door*s***
One **teacher**	Ten **teacher*s***

Table-4

Singular Number that tells us of 'One'	*Plural Number that tells us of 'More than One'*
One **girl**	Two **girl*s***
One **boy**	Three **boy*s***
One **window**	Four **window*s***
One **door**	Five **door*s***
One **teacher**	Ten **teacher*s***

Table-5

Singular Number that tells us of 'One'	*Plural Number that tells us of 'More than One'*
Man	Men
Child	Children
Tooth	Teeth
Foot	Feet
Ox	Oxen
Louse	Lice
Mouse	Mice
I	We
He/she/it	They

8. Pronouns to Denote 'One' or 'More' (Numbers)

(34) The words used in place of names are called **'Pronouns.'**

- We use **I, he, she, it, we, you, they** so that we don't have to repeat the names of people, places, or things.
- We use **I, He, She,** and **It** in place of the *names of only one person*.
- We use **We, You,** and **They** instead of the *names of more than one person.*
- **'This'** is used for an object that is nearby.
- **'That'** is used for an object that is far away. (one object)
- **'These'** is used for objects that are nearby.
- **'Those'** is used for objects that are far away. (more than one object)

(35) **Choose the words in brackets to replace the naming words in bold in the following sentences, and rewrite them in the blank spaces.**

1. **Raju** went to school. (He / She)
   = ____________________________________
2. **The girls** were there. (She/They)
   = ____________________________________
3. **Anu and I** will come. (We/You)
   = ____________________________________
4. Will **Sita** come too? (she/it)

= ____________________

5. Give the **cat** two biscuits. (me/it)

= ____________________

(36) **Use a pronoun instead of the underlined nouns or names, and submit the copy to your teacher.**

1. Ram is a good student. **Ram** is also a good athlete.

= ____________________

2. The boys were reading. But in the evening, **the boys** were playing.

= ____________________

3. Sudha plays badminton. **Sudha** also plays table tennis.

= ____________________

4. The horses were grazing. Then the **horses** came back.

= ____________________

5. Harish went to the hospital. **Harish** returned home when Harish got well.

= ____________________

(37) **Write 'This' or 'These' to fill in the blanks:**

1. ____________is a chair.
2. ____________ are chairs.
3. ____________ is a sandwich.
4. ____________ are things.
5. ____________ are children.
6. ____________ is the place where I was born.
7. ____________ are houses made of mud.
8. ____________ are pants I bought last year.

(38) **Fill the gap with 'That' or 'Those.'**

1. ____________is a picture I drew yesterday.
2. ____________ are our men.
3. ____________ eggs are spoilt.
4. ____________ socks are mine.
5. ____________ tree is very long.
6. ____________ woman is my aunt.
7. ____________ people were unknown.

(39) **Look at the picture given below. Write a sentence using *a pronoun* to answer each question about the image.**

Questions:

1. What is the boy doing? = ______________________________
2. What is the girl doing? = ______________________________
3. Where is the monkey? = ______________________________
4. What is the color of the sky? = ______________________________
5. What are the old man and the old woman doing? =

____

6. What are the birds doing? = ______________________________

9. Use of Describing Words or Adjectives

(40) **Describing words tells us more about naming words.**

- They give more information about people, places, or things.

- They tell us how an animal or a thing looks, feels, sounds, smells, or tastes (i.e., its size, color, number, hot, cold, course, pleasant, good, bad, sweet or bitter, and thus many more.)
- Describing words has their opposites too. **Examples:** Black-White, Tall-Short, Thick-Thin, etc.

(41) **Circle the describing words in each sentence.**

1. The brave fireman rescued the cat from the burning house.
2. My friends and I are going to watch a scary movie.
3. My friend likes to read funny books about fairies.
4. Our teacher is brilliant.
5. My purple sock has a hole in it.
6. Does loud music hurt your ears?

(42) **Circle the describing word and underline the names.**

Full moon

Evil witch

Big pumpkin

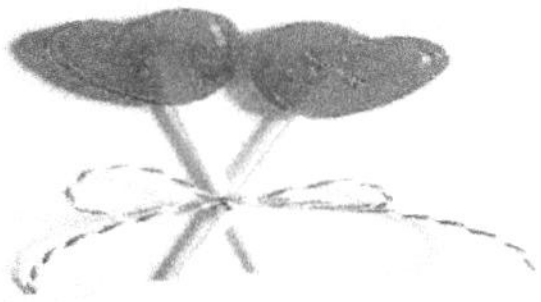

Sweet candy

Green Monster

Spooky house

Black bat

Pale vampire

Fun costume

(43) Write the opposites of the following words.

Wet ______________	Light ______________
Dark ______________	Heavy ______________
Clean ______________	Black ______________
Hot ______________	Long ______________
Rich ______________	Fat ______________

Look at the pictures and tick the correct sentences.

	The train is fast. ( )	The train is slow. ( )
	The moon is half. ( )	The moon is full. ( )
	Winters are hot. ( )	Winters are cold. ( )
	The car is red. ( )	The car is white. ( )
	The wood is hard. ( )	The wood is soft. ( )
	Chips taste salty. ( )	The chips taste sweet. ( )

(44) Complete the following sentences by describing words given in the box.

[domestic, torn and dirty, old, large]

1. Ours is a ____________ school.
2. The cow is a ____________ animal.
3. An ____________ man was walking with a stick.
4. The beggar was wearing ____________ clothes.

10. When describing words are used in Comparison

(45) **Comparison or degrees of Describing Adjectives:**

- When comparing two things or men or places, we generally add ***'-r'*** or ***'-er'*** *to the describing words,* and **'than'** is used after the word.
- When comparing more than two things, men or places, we generally add ***'-est'*** *to the describing words,* and article **'the'** is used before the word.
- The above form of describing words or adjectives (when compared between two) is called **Comparative Degree**, and
- When a comparison is made among more than two, the form of adjectives or describing words is called **Superlative Degree.**
- Sometimes, we use **'more'** or **'most'** to show a comparison between two or more.
- When there is no comparison between or among, the normal form of describing a word is called **Positive Degree.**
-

(46) **Study the examples.**

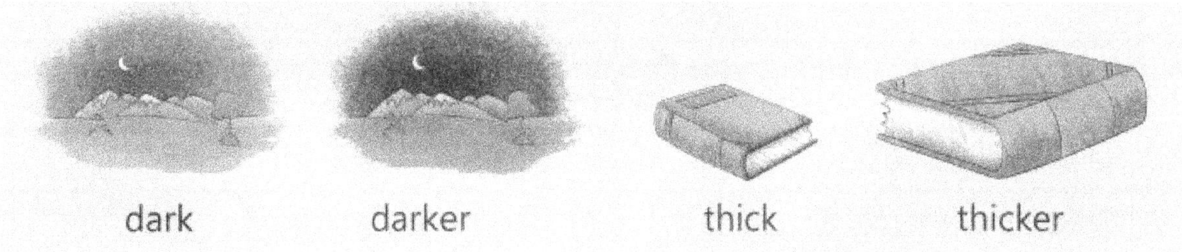

Read, when we use **'More' before a describing word**, generally after a longer word.

Examples:-

beautiful

more beautiful

active — **more** active
charming — **more** charming
cheerful — **more** cheerful
comfortable — **more** comfortable
delicious — **more** delicious

(47) **Read the picture story.**

"Do you like this big dining table?" Harshabardhan asks. "Wow! That's great. This is bigger than the one at our home," says Rita.

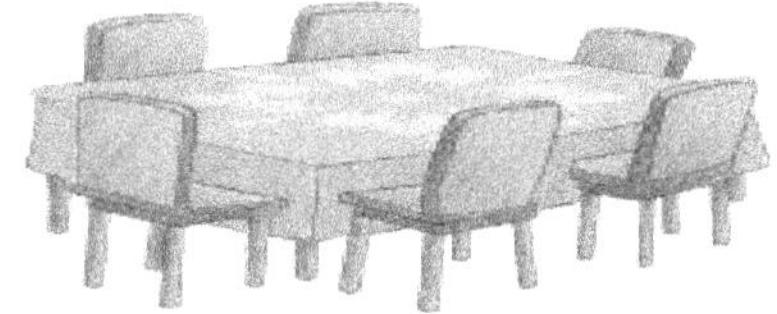

"Do you like the tablecloth?" asks Harsha. "Well... I must say it is more beautiful and prettier than the table," says Rita.

"Shall we buy it? It's not so expensive. It is cheaper than the other tables we saw," asks Rita. "Okay, let's ask the shopkeeper," says Harsha.

A. Answer the following questions.

1. Which word does Harsha use to describe the table?
2. Which words does Rita use to describe the tablecloth?
3. Is the table expensive?

B. Write the positive forms of words given below.

1. ____________ = bigger
2. ____________ = more beautiful
3. ____________ = prettier
4. ____________ = more expensive
5. ____________ = cheaper
6. ____________ = costlier

(48) Circle the correct describing word for each picture.

(49) Write the *correct form of the describing word*, along with its preposition, *'than,'* where necessary. You may also use 'more' where required.

1. Ram is ____________ Rita. (tall)

2. A pen is ____________ a sword. (useful)
3. Sarita is ____________ her sister. (young)

4. This dress is ____________ that dress. (beautiful)
5. Mangoes are ____________ apples. (cheap)

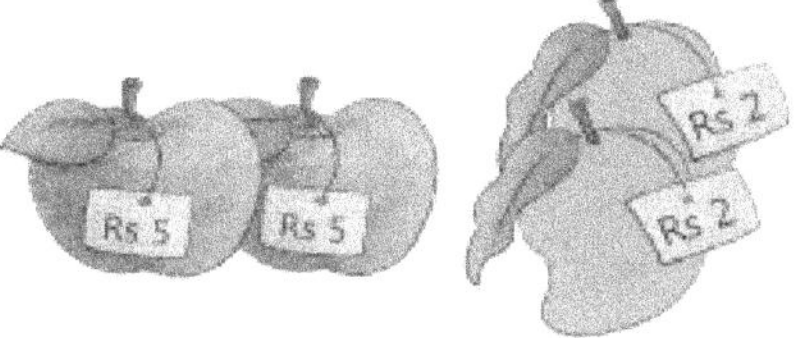

6. Iron is ____________ wood. (heavy)
7. Mr. Thakur was ____________ Mr. Paul. (wealthy)

8. A car runs ____________ a bicycle. (fast)

11. The use of *'All' and 'Few'* before naming words

(50) **'All' and 'Few'–describing words denoting the number of Nouns.**

- Some describing words tell how many people, places, animals, or things exist. They are called **describing words of numbers.**
- ***All*** and ***few*** are two examples of describing number words.

(51) Read the picture story.

Nine girls from our class are selected for the Annual Day function.

Three girls are selected for the dance performance, two girls are chosen for the solo performance, and four girls are selected to participate in the debate competition.

Only a few participants will receive distinguished prizes. However, participation certificates will be given to all the selected girls.

A. Answer the following questions as per the story.

1. How many girls are selected for solo performance?

____

2. How many girls are selected for dance performance?

____

3. Which describing words of number are used to represent the selected girls of the class?

____

B. Quick Prompts

1. How many months are there in a year? __________
2. How many days are there in a week? __________

3. How many players are there in a cricket team? ____________
4. How many colors does a traffic light have? ____________
5. How many colors are there in a rainbow? ____________

C. Underline the describing number words in the following sentences.

1. I have three books.
2. He ate a few bananas.
3. Kishore drank two glasses of milk.
4. A house has four walls.
5. All the students were present.

12. Use of *my, your, his, her, our, their, its,* etc.

(52) **Some describing words that show that something belongs to someone or something, etc.**

- Some describing words are also derived from Pronouns, such as ***my, your, his, her, our, their***, **its,** etc.
- The above forms show that something belongs to someone or something.

Read the picture story.

We are going to celebrate a party. "My idea is to serve egg sandwiches," says Rohit. "I like his idea because eggs are pretty easy to cook," says Varun.

"My idea is to serve cheeseburgers," says Nancy. "Does anyone else have a better idea?" asks Rohit. "Bunny, tell us your idea if you have any?" says Nancy.
"Everyone wants their favorite dish. However, I like chicken curry," says Bunny.
"Hey, don't forget Manu and Richa. They also have an idea for the party to serve pizzas," says Varun.
"I like pizza. It's my favorite food. I like their idea", says Nancy.

"I think I like Bunny's idea," says Rohit.

A. Answer the following questions as per the story.

1. What food does Rohit suggest for the party?
2. Who likes Manu and Richa's suggestion?
3. What do you think, whose suggestion is the best?

B. Write the name of the food the boys prefer for their party.

1. Manu and Richa ____________
2. Bunny ____________
3. Rohit ____________
4. Varun ____________
5. Nancy ______________

C. Fill in the blanks with 'my,' 'your,' 'his,' 'her,' 'him,' 'its,' 'our,' or **'their.'**

1. Would you lend me _________ book?
2. Return Madhu _________ book.
3. You and Madhu, submit _________ projects with the class teacher by tomorrow.
4. Nandita has lost ____________ purse.
5. The machine is useless without ___________ cord.
6. Hari, Raju, and Reena; ask them to be here with ____________ parents.
8. We love ____________ team.
9. The boy has given ____________ test.
10. My daughter has put on ____________ shoes
11. Ask __________ to be here in time.
12. Return me ___________ test book.

13. The use of *'A,'* *'An'* & *'The'* before Nouns

- 'A' and 'An' introduce a naming word.
- We use 'A' and 'An' to talk about one person, animal, or thing.
- We use 'A' when the first letter of the naming word is consonant.

- We use 'An' when the first letter of the naming word is a vowel.
- 'The' is used before special or particular names.

A. Circle the correct article (a/an/the) in each sentence.

1. Angelika wanted to read ________ (a/an) comic book.
2. He likes to read ________ (an/the) stories written by his mother.
3. Edward put ________ (a/an) orange on the table.
4. My mom made ________ (an/the) cake for me.

B. Write the correct article (a, an, the) before each naming word.

1. ______________ igloo
2. ______________ bench
3. ______________ banana
4. ______________ tree
5. ______________ inch
6. ______________ owl
7. ______________ tiger
8. ______________ eagle

Exercise

Fundamentals

- We said the article **'a'** is used before a noun begins with a consonant, and 'an' is used before a noun begins with a vowel.

- But, we use 'an' before a word begins with the silent 'h.' Examples:- **an Honest, an Hour**, etc.; the words are pronounced like '...onest,' and '...our,' like a vowel sound.
- And, when the initial vowel of the noun is pronounced like **'eu'/'you'** or **'oya,'** we use the article **'a'** before the word in place of 'an'; as, ***Examples:*** **'a uniform,' 'a eucalyptus tree,'** etc.

- 'The' is also used before a naming word that has already been talked about or the name of a specific/particular thing.

PRESENTATION

Read the picture story.

"I met **a** boy on my way to school," says Rahul.

The boy had **an** apple and **a** mango with him.

He gave **the** apple to me and ate **the** mango himself.

A. Answer the following questions as per the story.

1. Name the fruits that the boy had.
2. Which fruit did Rahul eat?
3. Which fruit did the boy eat?

B. Complete the sentences by writing *'a', 'an',* or *'the'* in the blanks.

1. ____________ tortoise and ____________ hare were neighbors. One day, ____________ hare challenged ____________ tortoise to ____________ race. However, finally, tortoise won ____________ race.

2. I have ____________ dog and ____________ parrot as pets. _______ dog is always quiet, but ____________ parrot is noisy.

C. Write a few sentences about each picture. Remember, 'a' and 'an' are to be used when writing about one naming word, and use 'the' when you repeat the name.

Example

This is a girl.
The girl is carrying a bag.
The bag looks heavy.

A

B

C

D. Write 'a' and 'an' before each of these words. Pay attention to the sound and not just the first letter.

1. ______________ European
2. ______________ house
3. ______________ useless dress
4. ______________ umbrella
5. ______________ unicorn
6. ______________ hour and a half
7. ______________ unhappy man
8. ______________ honest boy

14. Verbs (am, is, are, has, have & Doing Words)

- The words which show what someone or something is doing are called action words.
- Action words are also called doing words.
- Examples: **eat, sleep, dance, sing, run, fly, clap, touch, walk, play** etc.
- **Is, Am, Are** –are the different ways of saying **'be.'**
    - **'Is'** is used with 'he,' 'she,' 'it,' (third-person singular number)
    - **'Am'** is used with 'I' (First-person singular number) and

- **'Are'** is used with 'we,' 'you,' and 'they.' (1st., 2nd and 3rd person plural number and also 2nd person singular number)

- We use **'Has' and 'Have'** *to show that a thing belongs to someone.*
- We use **'Have'** with **'I,' 'we'**, and **'they.'** Examples: I have, We have, They have.
- **'Has'** is used *only with the third person singular number*, as Ram has, Willow has, etc.
- **'Have'** is used for more than one, *with first and second-person singular and plural and third-person plural numbers.*

A. Fill in the blanks with Is/Am/Are.

1. My father ____________ a taxi driver.
2. Andrea ____________ your music teacher.
3. My grandparents ____________ old.
4. I ____________ hungry.
5. Nicole & Elias ____________ friends.
6. We ____________ good friends.
7. It ____________ cool in spring.
8. The apples ____________ red.
9. My school bag ____________ green.
10. Rita ____________ my friend.

B. Fill in the blanks with 'has' or 'have.'

1. Sharks ____________ sharp teeth.
2. Insects ____________ six legs.
3. The parrot ____________ wings.
4. Birds ____________ feathers.
5. My school bag ____________ three pockets.
6. Rita ____________ a bicycle.
7. They ____________ a bungalow in the town.
8. I ____________ no bicycle to go with you.

C. Fill in the blanks with the appropriate verb form.

1. A whale __________ a very big animal. (is/are)
2. Your nails __________ long. (is/are)

3. The girls ___________ playing. (is/are)
4. An apple ___________ good to eat. (is/are)
5. I ___________ going there. (am/are)
6. I ___________ a student of class II. (am/are)
7. Laxmi ___________ a tall girl. (is/are)
8. Mita and Rita ___________ good friends. (is/are)

Identify the pictures with proper doing words:

A. Look at the pictures and put a (X) mark against wrong answers.

(1) Eating food ( ); Cooking food ( )

(2) Playing cricket ( ); Playing football ( )

(3) Barking (   ); Yawning (   )

(4) Happy Birthday ( ); Happy New Year ( )

B. Look at the pictures and fill in the blanks with verbs given within brackets.

(punch, taste, walk, catch, see, hear, eat, smell)

You ____________ with your tongue. You ____________ with your fist.

You ____________ with your hands. You ____________ with your nose.

You __________ with your ears. You __________ with your legs.

You __________ with your eyes. You __________ with your mouth.

Use of '–s,' '–es' to the verbs

Fundamentals

- **'–s,'** or **'–es' verb forms** are used *only with the third person singular number of the subject* in the sentence.
- The **'–s'** and **'–es' verb forms** *are not used with the plural number of the subject*,
- When the doing word ends with **'–e,'** generally, the **'–s' verb form is used.**
- If the doing word ends with a consonant or double consonant **(except '–ch'),** the **'–es' verb form is used.** (And there are other exceptions.)

A. Fill in the blanks with the correct word.

1. She __________ the best chocolate cake in the school. (bake/bakes)
2. Cats __________ mice. (chase/chases)
3. They __________ to bed at 10 pm. (go/goes)
4. Amit __________ the answer to the question. (know/knows)
5. Anu __________ a lot of work. (has/have)
6. They like to __________ jigsaw puzzles. (do/does)

The use of Progressive form in the Present time

Fundamentals

- To talk about *actions that are still going on presently*, we use **the doing word + ing.**
- **'Is,' 'Am,'** and **'are'** are used as helping words before them.
- **Examples:** I am studying. He is swimming. They are reading, etc.

PRESENTATION

Read the picture story.

Nancy is visiting her grandparents. At this moment, she is sitting on her grandfather's knee, listening to a story. She loves her grandfather's story very much.

Mr. Gopal is Nancy's grandfather. He is holding her hands. They are sitting in the living room. Right now, he is telling her a story. They enjoy each other's company.

Mrs. Gopal is Nancy's grandmother. She is standing in the kitchen and baking cookies for Nancy and her grandfather. She is also listening to the story.

A. Answer the following questions.

1. Who is Nancy visiting today? ______________

2. Where are Mr. Gopal and his granddaughter sitting? ______________
3. What is Mrs. Gopal doing? ______________

B. Fill in the blanks with the *–ing form of the verb* from the story above.

- Visit ______________ Hold ______________ Listen ______________
- Live ______________ Tell ______________ Stand ______________
- Sit ______________ Bake ______________

C. Add 'ing' to the following doing words. *(Remove the letter 'e' from the verb before adding '-ing' if the verb ends with '-e')*

- Come ______________ Run ______________ Ask ______________
- Sleep ______________ Catch ______________ Fall ______________
- Meet ______________ Jump ______________ Drop ______________
- Bring ______________ Climb ______________ Live ______________
- Go ____________ Slide ____________ Move ____________
- Cook ____________ Sit ____________ Stand ____________
- Write ____________ Read ____________ Play ____________

C. Fill in the blanks with the correct doing word and helping verb. (present continuous = am/is/are + –ing doing word)

1. They ______________ the roller-coaster ride. (enjoy)
2. Jiya ______________ her hair. (wash)
3. It ______________ dark. (get)
4. The dentist ______________ Suman's teeth. (examine)
5. The train ______________ through the tunnel. (pass)

D. Match the pictures with the correct actions and tick the right box.

1.	• Friends are hugging. [ ] • Nancy is hanging posters. [ ] • The clown is performing. [ ]

• Lata is walking to school. [ ] • Payal is blowing a bubble.[ ] • A dog is hopping. [ ]	2.
3.	• Rita is standing in a queue. [ ] • Meena is listening to music. [ ] • The ball is hitting his head. [ ]
• The ducks are quacking. [ ] • Rahul is collecting the leaves.[ ] • Bella is baking a yummy cake.[ ]	4.
5.	• Han is tying his shoelaces. [ ] • Reena is painting a picture. [ ] • Rahul is kissing her mother. [ ]
• Raju is shutting the door. [ ] • Sohan is rushing to work. [ ] • Mita is working hard. [ ]	6.

The use of Past Forms of Verbs

Fundamentals

- Doing words also talk about something that happened in the past.
- Here, doing words end with **-ed** or **-d.**
- **Walk- walked, Sail- sailed, Dance- danced, Chase- chased.**
- Sometimes, we change the spelling of the doing word.
- **Sing-Sang, Fly-Flew, Sit-Sat, Write-Wrote, etc.**
- Sometimes, we change the doing word completely.

- **Go-Went, Tell-Told, Teach-Taught, Buy-Bought, Eat-Ate, Do-Did**
- Sometimes, we do not change the doing word; like, **Burst-Burst, Cut-Cut, Hit-Hit**

PRESENTATION

Read the picture story.

Last week, Bunny baked a cake for Lilly's birthday party. Lilly wanted a strawberry cake with pink frosting.

First, Bunny mixed the ingredients in a big bowl and baked the cake for 20 minutes. He prepared the pink frosting. Lastly, he wrote Lilly's name on top with white frosting. Last, he put seven candles on the cake.

On Sunday, Bunny surprised Lilly with the strawberry cake. Lilly loved her cake! Lilly got many gifts on her birthday. But Lilly said that the cake was the best gift of them all!

A. Answer the following questions from the story above.

1. What did Bunny do for Lilly's birthday party?
2. What did Bunny prepare?
3. What did Lilly like best among her birthday gifts?

B. Add -ed to the following doing words. Remember, *when the word ends with '-e,'* add only '-d' to the doing word.

Bake _______________

Prepare _______________

Love _______________

Want _______________

Mix _______________

Surprise _______________

C. Complete each sentence by adding -ed to the doing words given in the brackets.

1. My dad (craft) _______________ a boat.
2. He (mow) _______________ the grass.
3. I (watch) _______________ television in the morning.
4. Sameer (pick) _______________ up the journal today.
5. We (serve) _______________ lunch at 12.30.
6. Grandma (bake) _______________ the best cookies.
7. He (paint) _______________ the house.
8. Sarika (cook) _______________ the breakfast.
9. Pawan (play) _______________ the piano at the concert.
10. I _______________ (open) my book yesterday.

D. Circle the doing word with -ed in the following passage.

I lived in a tent. I washed and bathed in a stream. I cooked my food. I watched cute little rabbits playing near my tent. I walked through the forest. I climbed up to the top of a hill. There, I collected some rare flowers. I dried them and pasted them in my flower book. I enjoyed it a lot.

E. Change all the doing words to show that the things happened in the past. Rewrite the sentences in the blanks.

1. She wants to wear a new dress. = ____
2. Anjan sings beautifully. = ____
3. They try to break into the house. = ____

4. We write in our notebooks. = ______________________________
5. I go to the playground. = ______________________________
6. We play hide and seek. = ______________________________
7. He seems to be angry. = ______________________________
8. You know the truth. = ______________________________
9. Sanjay shouts for help. = ______________________________
10. It starts raining heavily. = ______________________________

F. Add –ed to the following words.

Slip __________	Drop __________
Want __________	Clean __________
Carry __________	Mark __________
Play __________	Discover __________
Dance __________	Spot __________
Tag __________	Step __________

The use of 'Was' and 'Were'

Fundamentals

- The verbs **was** and **were** are also the forms of the verb **'To Be.'**
- We use ***was*** and ***were*** to show the state of the past that existed or happened in the past.
- We use **'was'** with **he, she,** and **it.**
- We use **'were'** with **we, you,** and **they.**
- Often, a past time is meant using words like– ***yesterday, last night, last week, last month,*** and ***last year.***

Presentation

Read the picture story.

A. Answer the following questions from the story given above.

1. What did the children do in the snowfall? ______________
2. What did the people wear in Manali? ______________
3. Was the hotel room cold or warm? ______________

B. Fill in the blanks with 'was' or 'were.'

It ________ holiday yesterday. The school ______________ closed and the shops ________ closed. We ______________ at home. It ______________ fun.

C. Fill in the blanks with 'was' or 'were.'

1. We ______________ the champions last year.
2. I ______________ in class I last year.
3. Mom and Dad ______________ were on vacation last week.
4. The weather ______________ fine this morning.
5. There ______________ a lot of people at our party yesterday.
6. There ______________ a small lake here many years ago.
7. He ______________ sick yesterday.
8. Don't blame him. It ______________ my mistake.

D. Write was or were in the blank spaces in the following passage.

It ______________ a beautiful day, and there ______________ not a cloud in the sky. Mom, Dad, and I ______________ in the garden. Dad ______________ in the vegetable garden planting some seeds, and Mom and I ______________ busy with other jobs. The sun ______________ hot and soon I ______________ feeling very tired. Mom and Dad ______________ not tired at all. They went on working for a long time. I ______________ glad when it ______________ time to go inside and have a drink together.

(53) **Fill in the blanks with is, am, are, was, were.**

1. Tom ______________ in the garden yesterday.

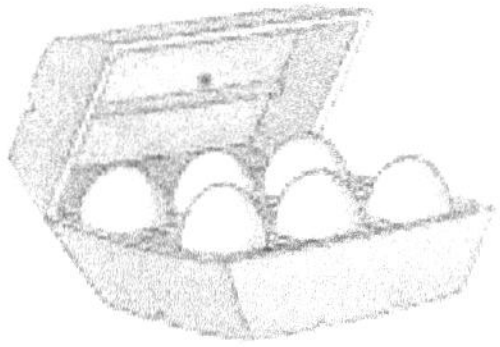

2. The eggs ______________ in the box now.

3. Sugar ______________ the packet.

4. There ______________ hot coffee in the cup.

5. The cookies ______________ on the table now.

6. Three potatoes ______________ on the table.

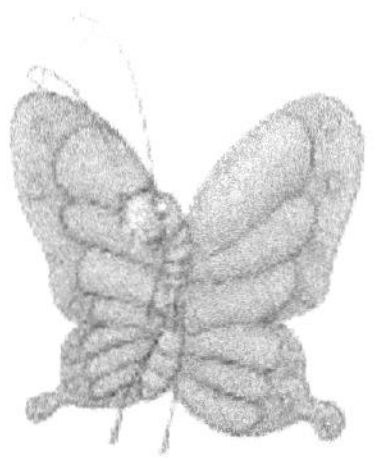

7. The butterfly ____________ very beautiful.

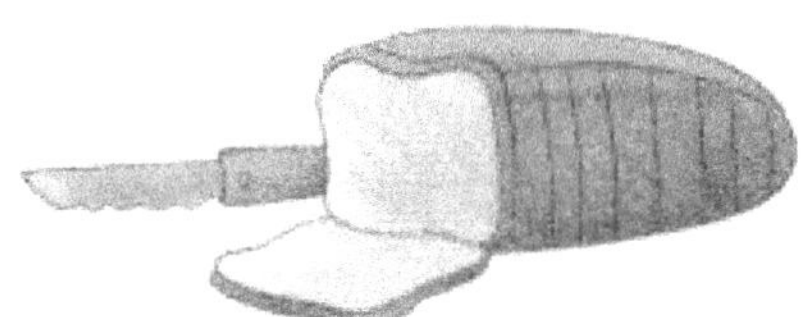

8. The bread and knife ____________ on the table.

9. The teapot ____________ full yesterday.

10. There ____________ three apples on the branch.

11. I ____________ writing the blackboard yesterday.

12. The bottle ____________ full of milk yesterday.

13. There ____________ two apples in the kitchen.

14. Bill ____________ crying now.

15. Paul ______________ rowing the boat two hours ago.

16. Pam ______________ sitting on the floor now.

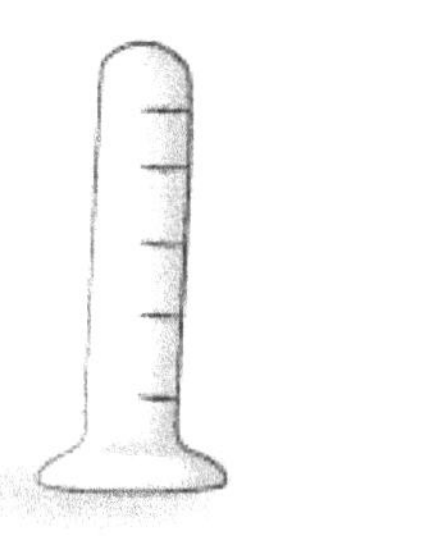

17. It ______________ very hot yesterday.

18. It ______________ raining today.

19. The books ______________ new.

20. Mona ______________ cooking now.

The Use of 'had'

Fundamentals

- Had is also followed by naming words.
- Had is used to show that something belonged to someone or some other thing in the past.
- We use **'Had'** to say what we ate or drank.
- We use **'Had'** for things that happened to people or affected them in the past.
- We use **'had'** when we talk about wishes. **I wish I had a new bike.**

PRESENTATION

Read the picture story.

Last night, Mona and Sonu danced in a competition. They had practiced for six months before the competition, and they were very good.

Mona and Sonu's friends were ¡ in the audience. Before that night, they had never seen Mona and Sonu's dance.

After everyone had danced, the judges announced the winners. Mona and Sonu won! They were the best dancers ¡n the competition. Mona was glad they had practiced a lot.

A. Answer the following questions.

1. What did Mona and Sonu do in the competition?

____

2. Who was present in the audience?

____

3. What did the judges announce at the end of the competition?

____

EXERCISE

A. Use the 'had' and '- ed' forms of verbs along with other forms of verbs, like, **past and progressive tense in the past where necessary, to complete the following sentences.** (The use of past perfect tense is when an action was completed in the past.)

1. When their mother _____________ (come) home last night, the children _____________ (eat) their dinner.
2. Yesterday I _____________ (see) a woman who _____________ (be) at school with my grandfather. Wasn't it strange?
3. It started to rain, and I _____________ (remember) that I _____________ (forget) to close my bedroom window.
4. I _____________ (find) a book that I never _____________ (read).

B. Fill in the blanks using the verbs 'Had' and **'–ed' forms at the end of the doing verbs.**

1. When I arrived at the cinema, the film _____________ (start).
2. She _____________ (live) in China before she went to Thailand.
3. After they _____________ (eat) the shellfish, they began to feel sick.
4. If you _____________ (listen) to me, you would have got the job.
5. After we _____________ (finish) dinner, we went out.

15. How Words or Adverbs

Fundamentals

- Words that tell us more about doing words are called **How Words.**

- It shows how an action is done. Look at the examples given below.

Read the following sentences.

The girl sang **sweetly**. The baby cried **loudly**. Anand wrote **neatly**.

In the above examples

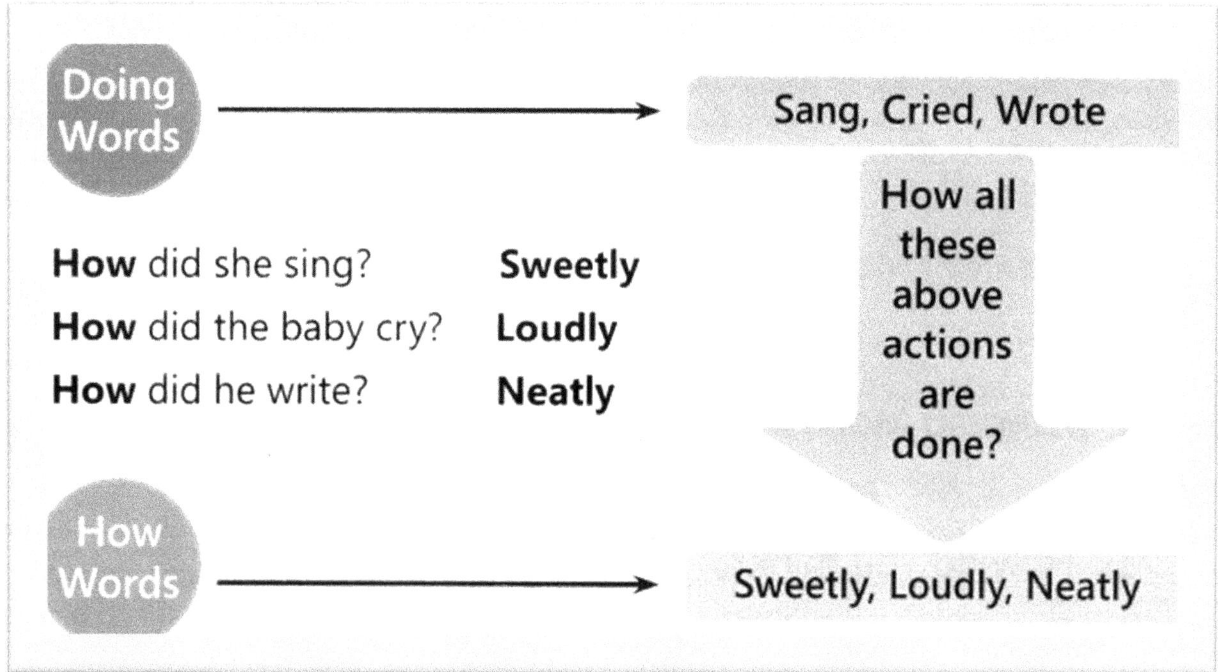

How Words end in-ly. Look at the examples.

Slow – slowly,	*Loud – loudly,*	*Brave – bravely,*	*Sweet – sweetly,*	*Sad – sadly,*	*Quick – quickly,*
Bright – brightly,	*Kind – kindly,*	*Right– rightly,*	*Bad – badly,*	*Wise– wisely,*	*Happy – happily*

PRESENTATION

Read the picture story.

Mohit has enthusiastically participated in the Writing Olympiad. He practiced for this competition seriously.

He practiced silently. During the competition, he wrote slowly and neatly. He used his words artistically.

Humbly and Kindly, the Judges announced the result, with Mohit as the winner. "Well Done! Mohit." Mohit accepted his trophy happily.

A. Answer the following questions from the story above.

1. How did Mohit practice? ______________
2. How did Mohit write? ______________
3. How did Mohit accept the trophy? ______________

B. Describe the way you do things.

1. How do you think? ______________
2. How do you fight? ______________

3. How do you sing? ______________
4. How do you dance? ______________
5. How do you walk? ______________

C. Look at the pictures. Choose the correct 'How' Word from the box to fill in the blanks.

neatly, angrily, quickly, sadly, slowly, heavily, happily, brightly, loudly, beautifully

1. Laugh ______________
2. Run ______________ 
3. Shout ______________ 
4. Sun ______________ 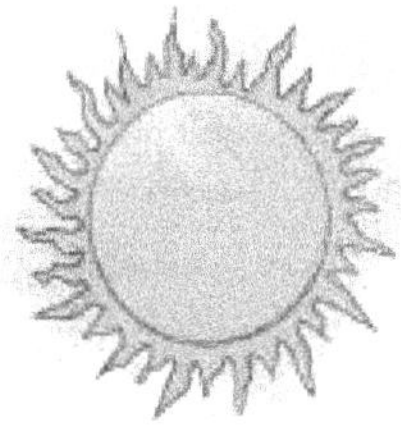
5. Walk ______________

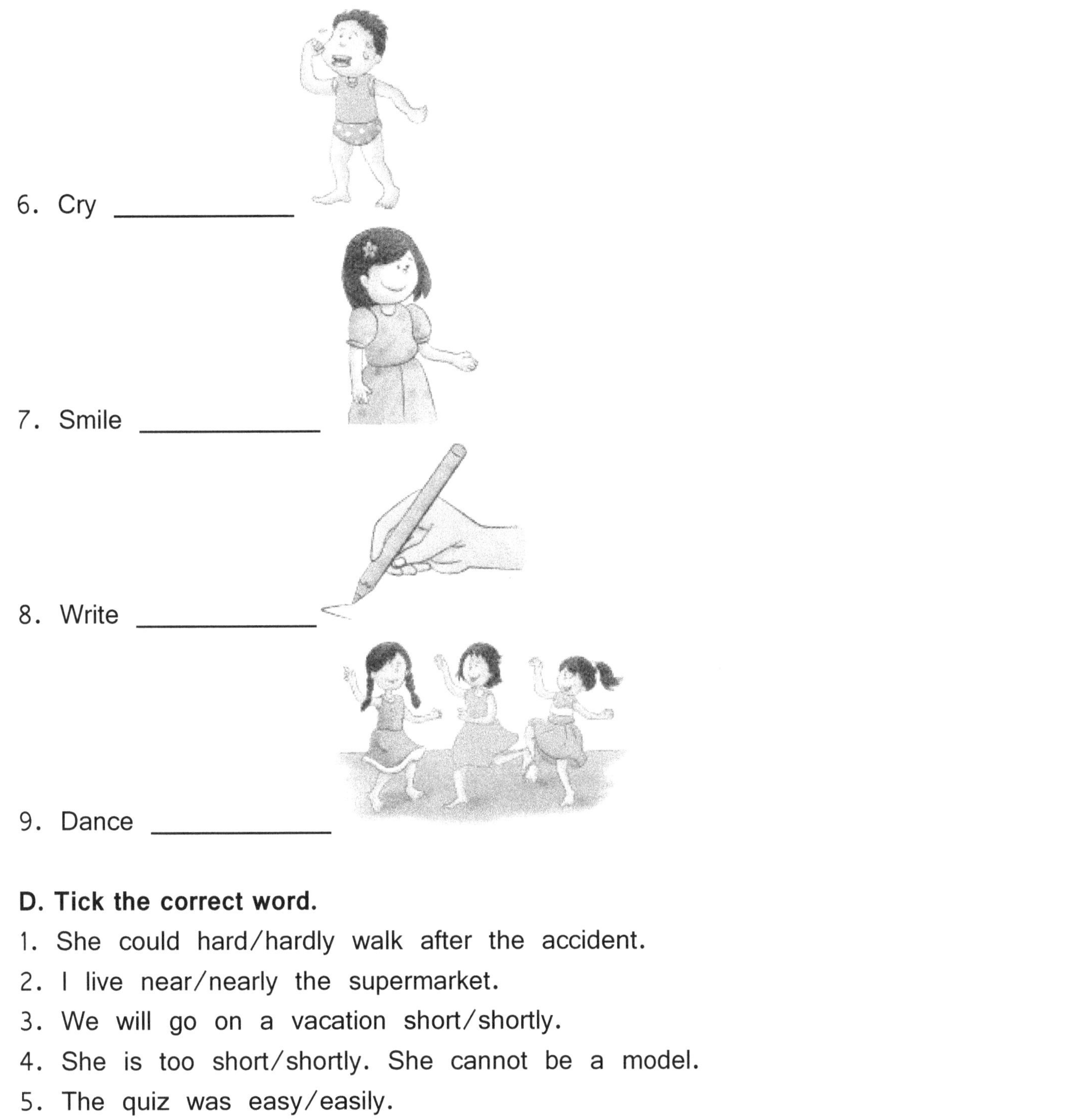

6. Cry ____________

7. Smile ____________

8. Write ____________

9. Dance ____________

D. Tick the correct word.

1. She could hard/hardly walk after the accident.
2. I live near/nearly the supermarket.
3. We will go on a vacation short/shortly.
4. She is too short/shortly. She cannot be a model.
5. The quiz was easy/easily.

[Submit the copy with your teacher.]

E. Make 'how words' by adding -ly: For example: Slow – <u>Slowly</u>

1. Careful – ____________
2. Quick – ____________
3. Loud – ____________
4. Terrible – ____________

5. Weak – ______________

6. Happy – ______________

F. Choose the correct option to complete the sentences.

1. I like to live in a ___________ house. clean ( )/cleanly ( )

2. Rashi usually sings ___________. happy ( )/happily ( )

3. Madhuri is a ___________ girl. beautiful ( )/ beautifully ( )

4. Reena speaks English ___________. fluent ( )/fluently ( )

5. Sahil ran ___________ fast ( ) / fastly ( )

16. 'Where Words,' 'When Words' & Prepositions

'Where words' or 'Prepositions' are words that are used before a naming word and show the relation between two words in the sentence. Thus, they denote the place of an action.

Where Words tell where something or someone is placed.

In, on, above, below, under, and **at** are all Where Words.

A. Underline the 'Where Words' in the following sentences.

1. A bird was flying above in the sky.
2. The ball rolled under a car.
3. She put the letter in her pocket.
4. I left the book on the table.
5. The crow is sitting below the tree.

(The answers to the above are **above, under, in, on,** and **below.**)

Note: The above 'Where Words' are also called **Prepositions.**

B. Use the following 'where words' in sentences of your own. The first one has been done for you.

Where Words	Sentence
1. IN	Please, come in.
2. ON	
3. AT	
4. BELOW	
5. UNDER	

C. Choose the correct prepositions to complete the sentences given below.

1. A newspaper is ____________ the pillow. (in, on, under)

2. A ball is ____________ the car. (in, on, under)

3. Clothes are ____________ the closet. (in, on, under)

4. A cat is ____________ the chair. (in, on, under)

5. Candy is ____________ the bag. (in, on, under)

6. Shells are ____________ the stool. (in, on, under)

Study more 'Where Words' or 'Prepositions'

Fundamentals: Where they are used and examples. Study the table.

Preposition	Use	Example
Across	From one side to the other side	You mustn't go across this road here.
Around	in a circular way	We're sitting around the campfire.
Behind	at the back of	Our house is behind the supermarket.
Between	is on each side	Our house is between the supermarket and the school.
Near	close to	Our house is near the supermarket.

Over	above	The cat jumped over the wall.
In front of	the part that is in the direction it faces	Our house is in front of the supermarket.
Next to	beside	Our house is next to the supermarket.

PRESENTATION

Read the picture story.

This is a picture of our sea beach trip. We went for a picnic at the beach. The crab was crawling near the sea, and the dolphin behind the boat was jumping out of the water.

On the beach, chairs were beside the table. The little girl was sitting in front of the sand castle, and the beach ball was lying between the girls.
Across the sea, the boy was in the parachute. The sun was shining above the sea.

A. Answer the following questions as per the story.

1. Where was the crab in the story?

____

2. Where was the beach ball?

____

3. What was behind the boat in the picture?

____

B. Look at the picture story again and state whether the following statements are true or false.

1. The dolphin is under the water. ____________
2. The crab is near the sea. ____________
3. The boat is below the tree. ____________
4. The little girl is in between the sandcastle. ____________

PRESENTATION–2

E. Study the picture and state whether the following statements are 'true' or 'false.'

1. The chair is next to the desk ____________________
2. The bed is opposite to the window. ____________
3. The computer is under the desk. ____________
4. The bookcase is on the wall. ____________
5. The bin is between the bed and the desk. ____________
6. The lamp is on the desk. ____________
7. The poster is above the shelf. ____________
8. The window is above the bed. ____________
9. The clock is on the bed. ____________

PRESENTATION–3

D. Look at the picture and fill in the blanks.

1. The carpet is on the floor.
2. The elephant poster is ____________ the wall.
3. The clothes are ____________ the wardrobe.
4. The photo is ____________ the clock and the plant.
5. The doll house is ____________ the wardrobe.
6. The bookcase is ____________ the sofa.
7. The shelf is ____________ the wardrobe.
8. The pencil cup is ____________ desk.
9. The chair is ____________ the desk.
10. The elephant poster is ____________ the panda poster.
11. The bag is ____________ the desk.

E. Fill in the following blanks with correct prepositions.

1. He climbed ____________ the hills.
2. My family usually eats dinner ____________ 8.00 pm.
3. Look ____________ the street before crossing.
4. There is a mango tree ____________ the lake.

5. My father took grapes ____________ of his bag.
6. The boy was standing ____________ the curtain.
7. The bench is ____________ the tree.
8. Neha and Vivek are playing ____________ of their house.
9. There is a fence ____________ the house.
10. We have beautiful flowers ____________ the garden.

Like 'where words,' there are also some **'when words'** that **denote the time of an action.** Study the following chart, where the words are used before:

IN	On	At
Month or Year. E.g., in February, in 2010	1. **Day** E.g., on Monday, on Republic Day, on my birthday	1. **Time of clock** E.g., at 5 O'clock, at 7:30 PM
The particular time of day, month, or year. E.g., in the morning, in the evening, in the first week of July, in summer, in winter, etc.	2. **Date** E.g., on 5th of March, March 5	2. **Short and precise time** E.g., at noon, at sunset, at lunchtime, at bedtime, at the moment, at the same time

17. Joining Words or Conjunctions

Fundamentals

A word that joins two sentences, sometimes two words of the same category or two clauses, is called a joining word.

'And,' 'But,' and **'Or'** are the words that join two parts of the sentences.

We use **'And'** to join two words or sentences.

We use **'But'** to join two different thoughts and ideas.

We use **'Or'** to join two parts of a sentence when there is a choice. It means that one of two things can happen.

Read the examples given below.

The boy **and** the girl are wearing hats.

I like ice cream, **but** I do not like milk.

I will have milk **or** honey.

PRESENTATION

Read the picture story.

Hummingbirds are small and colorful. Their legs are weak, but their wings are strong. Their wings beat fast and make a humming sound.

The birds can fly up or down, backwards or sideways. They can hang in the air and drink nectar from a flower.

They usually lay two eggs and their babies are featherless. Grass, bark or cobwebs hold their nest together. It's really amazing!

A. Answer the following questions as per the story.

1. Describe Hummingbirds? ______________________________

2. What have you learned about Humming bird's legs and wings from the story?
____

3. From where does Hummingbird drink nectar? ______________________________

B. Fill in each blank with a word from the story above.

1. Hummingbirds make a humming sound with their __________

2. Hummingbirds can fly up __________ down, backward __________ sideways.

3. __________, bark or __________ hold the nest together.

GRAMMAR EXERCISE:

A. Fill in the blanks with 'and' or 'but'

1. Vijay is tall __________ thin.

2. Raju is tall __________ not thin.

3. I found the book ____________ I can't find the pen.

4. I have found the book ____________ pen.

5. The dog ____________ the cat are fighting.

6. The dog is sleeping ____________ the cat is not.

B. Use 'or' to join the following. The first one has been done for you.

1. Do you like tea? Do you like coffee?

Answer: I like tea, but not coffee.

1. Is your shirt red? Is your shirt green?

Answer: ______________________________

2. Is that Meera? Is that Rita?

Answer: ______________________________

3. Is a tiger stronger? Is a lion stronger?

Answer: ______________________

4. Do you like a burger? Do you like a pizza?

Answer: ______________________

C. Complete the sentences with correct conjunctions.

1. My grandma makes tasty cakes __________ snacks for us all. **(and, but)**
2. Her writing is good, __________ her spellings are weak. **(and, but)**
3. Anuj __________ Sunny are playing on the beach. **(and, but)**
4. Rita fell down, __________ she did not get hurt. **(and, but)**

D. Circle the joining words in the following sentences.

1. They walked and played in the park.
2. I like popcorn, but my sister likes chips.
3. Mohit hoped to get a baseball or video game for his birthday.
4. Nina knocked at the door, but no one answered.
5. We saw clowns, horses, and elephants at the circus.
6. Who will go with us? Mita or Gita?

18. Interjection or words of expressing emotions

An Interjections is a part of speech that shows strong feelings, such as surprise, anger, or joy.

They are followed by an exclamation sign (!) or a comma (,).

- She shouted at him, “Go away! I hate you!”
- He exclaimed: “What a fantastic house you have!”
- “Good heavens!” he said, “Is that true?”

- "Help!"
- "Shut up!"
- "Stop!"

A. Put appropriate punctuation [comma (,)/ full stop (.) (full stop,)/exclamation marks (!), wherever necessary, in the following sentences.

1. Wow What a wonderful crowd
2. I'm so happy to see you
3. What a pleasant surprise
4. Look out
5. Ouch I've cut my finger
6. Oh no I've lost my bag
7. How hot it was
8. How exciting that was
9. Watch out

B. How many words can you think of that express how the children feel? Write your words in clouds. Don't forget the exclamation marks.

19. Opposite Words

- The **opposite words** are also known as **'antonyms.'**

- Words that ***have completely different meanings*** are called opposite words.

Study the list of opposite words.

above	below
absence	presence
active	lazy
afraid	brave
against	for
always	never
answer	question
awake	sleep
bad	good
beautiful	ugly
body	soul

bottom	top
brother	sister
clean	dirty
close	open
cool	warm
daughter	son
devil	angel
deep	shallow
distant	near
even	odd
far	near
fast	slow
female	male
friend	enemy
guest	host
hell	heaven
high	low
kind	cruel
less	more

A. Use the opposite of the underlined word and rewrite the sentences.

1. My teacher gives **<u>hard</u>** home tasks. = My teacher gives **easy** home tasks.

2. We live **far from** my grandmother. _____________ (near of)
3. Have you **lost** your pencil? _____________
4. School starts too **late**. _____________
5. My dog climbs **under** the fence. _____________
6. I like a **cold** lunch. _____________
7. Mohan is the **shortest** boy in your class. _____________
8. Today, it will be **warm** outside. _____________
9. Mita is **sad** about the party. _____________
10. I am **slow** at running the race. _____________

B. Match the words in column A with their opposites in column B:

A	B
a) Bad	1) Good
b) Bitter	2) Shallow
c) Begin	3) Awake
d) Build	4) Common
e) Bent	5) Destroy
f) Lend	6) Short
g) Worst	7) Sweet
h) Rare	8) Straight
i) Deep	9) Cruel
j) Sleep	10) Best
k) Kind	11) Borrow
l) Tall	12) End

20. Reading Skills: Unseen Passages

Picture Comprehension

Read the picture story:

Ria has a new bicycle. It is bright pink and shiny, and it was a gift from her uncle.

He hid it behind a bush to surprise her. Ria jumped with joy when she looked behind the bush and saw the bicycle.

She gave her uncle a big hug. She loves her new bicycle, and she loves her uncle.

A. Answer the following questions.

1. What is the color of the bicycle?
2. Who was it a gift from?
3. Where was it hidden?
4. What did Ria do when she saw the bicycle?

Picture Comprehension 2

Read the picture story.

The bookshelf in my house is tall and holds many books, some pictures, and candles. It has big and small books.

There are also books for kids and books for parents. There is a picture of my mother and father, too.

There are two blue candles and a yellow candle. I am glad the books I like are on the lowest shelf.

A. Write the answers to the questions.

1. What type is the bookshelf?
2. What is on the bookshelf?
3. Whose photograph is on the bookshelf?
4. What is the color of the candles?

Picture Comprehension 3

Read the picture story.

The Parade

My mother took me and my brother Arun to the fun parade on Monday.

I saw three pretty white horses walking and some big dogs running in the parade.

The clowns and their puppies had on purple hats and big orange pants.

After the parade, the clowns gave me candy to eat. I ate my candy, and I clapped and clapped. It was a fun parade to see with my brother and mother.

A. Answer the following questions.

1. When did the mother and Arun go for a parade? ________________
2. Who gave candies to the children? ________________
3. What was the clown's puppy wearing? ________________
4. What did they all see in the fun parade? ________________
5. Give the describing words used in the passage for the following words.

________________Horses, ________________Dogs,
________________Hats, ________________Pants.

Moral Comprehension Passages

Some passages end with teaching some true lessons of life. Such passages are called Moral passages.

Read the passage and answer the questions that follow.

There was a king in Scotland. His name was Robert Bruce. He fought many battles and won them. But once, he was badly defeated. He ran away from the battlefield to save his life. He took shelter in a cave where he hid himself. He

lost all hope for life.

But one day, he saw a spider trying to reach the roof of the cave, where it had a cobweb. It made six attempts to reach its web, but every time, it slipped down. He was surprised to see that the spider did not lose heart but continued its efforts to reach the top. At the seventh attempt, the spider was successful in reaching its web.

This incident boosted King Bruce's spirit. He gained new strength and fresh courage. He fought another battle and was ultimately successful in making his country free from his enemies.

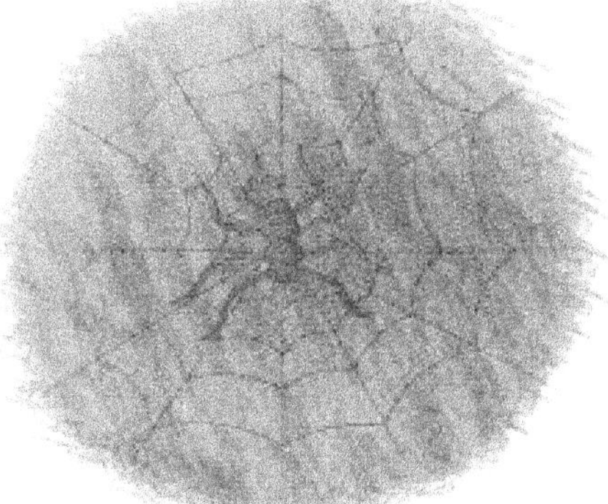

Moral: Keep trying until you succeed. The one who never stops making an effort is the one who ultimately wins.

Answer the following questions.

A. Arrange the jumbled words to make words.

1. bltate = Battle
2. mptsatte ________________
3. hlerste ________________
4. erdips ________________
5. bewcob ________________

B. Fill up the blanks.

1. King Bruce was the king of ________________
2. King took shelter in a ________________
3. He saw ________________ in the cave.
4. The spider was successful at the ________________ attempt.
5. The moral of the story is ________________________________.

C. State True/False.

1. The king's name was Robert Bruce. (   )
2. The king saw the lion in the cave. (   )
3. The spider made three attempts to reach its web. (   )
4. The spider incident boosted the spirit of the king. (   )
5. The moral of the story is 'Do Not Try Again'. (   )

D. Look at the picture and name it.

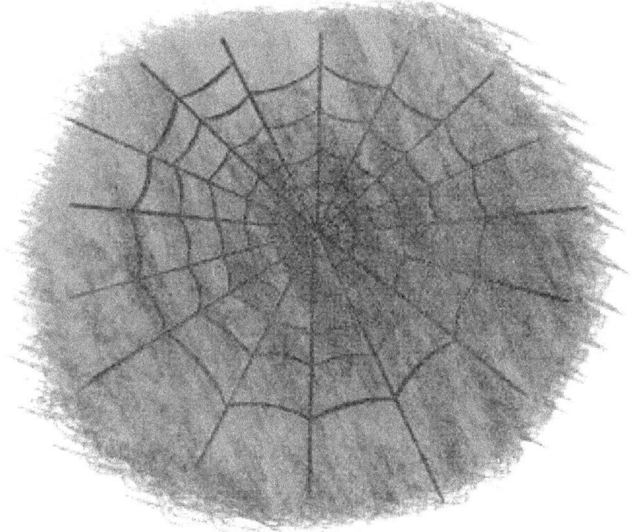

____

Poem Comprehension with Questions

Read the poem carefully and answer the following questions.

Snow School Today

We bundle ourselves for it's time to leave.
The wind whips as we wait for Mr. Steve.
He rounds the corner in the yellow bus.
Opening the door, he calls out for us,
"It's cold this morning! Get in! The heat's on!"
We wave our goodbyes, and then we are gone.
The trip this morning is a slippery ride.
Look out the window; snow falls outside.
The street lights are blurry and glowing like jewels.
Beneath all our boots, snow melts into pools.
Now safe at school, we hear Mr. Steve say,
"Hurry inside now and keep warm today!"

1. Who is Mr. Steve?

____

2. Which words best describe the weather in the poem?

    a. cold and rainy ( )
    b. snowing and calm ( )

c. windy and cold ( )
d. snowing and hailing ( )

3. The seventh line of the poem says:
The trip this morning is a slippery ride. What does this mean?
a. Kids are slipping when they get on the bus. ( )
b. The bus wheels are slipping on the ice. ( )
c. Kids are slipping and falling when they walk to the bus. ( )
d. The bus floor is slippery. ( )

4. Write three words to describe Mr. Steve. ________________, ________________ and ________________.

5. How do the students probably feel when they are on the bus?
a. colder ( )
b. warmer ( )
c. tired ( )
d. lost ( )

Nonfiction Passages

Passage-1

Read the passage and answer the following questions.

Going to the Movies

My class is going to the movies next week. We have to get permission slips signed before we go. We also need to ask our parents if they will drive us to the movie theatre. We are going to see a movie that tells the story of a book we read. We love it when movies are made from books. It is fun to compare movies to books. I usually like the book better. We get to the movie OUT early so we can buy popcorn. Some of us buy candy and slushes, too.

We all enjoy watching the movie. When we return to school, we talk about things that were in the movie and the book. The movie and book are similar, but we all agree that we like the book better. Books let you picture the characters any way you want.

Answer the following questions.

1. What do the students need to do before going to the movie?
2. What is fun to compare?
3. What do the students like better, the movie or the book?
4. What do the books let you do?

Nonfiction Passages: Passage-2

Read the passage and answer the following questions.

'T' Time with Elephants

Three interesting things about elephants begin with the letter T – trunk, tusk, and teeth. An elephant's trunk has over forty thousand muscles and tendons. The trunk is a combination of the nose and the upper lip. An elephant uses its trunk to pick up things. It also uses its trunk for smelling. An elephant has two tusks. The tusks are made of ivory. The tusks grow from the elephant's upper jaw. An elephant has these two "teeth" instead of incisor teeth. The tusks grow throughout an elephant's life. An elephant uses its tusks to drill for water and to dig up food. All African elephants have tusks. Only some Asian male elephants have tusks. Some female Asian elephants also have tusks, which are very small and hidden inside their mouth.

An elephant also has four other teeth. These teeth are molars. An elephant has one upper molar and one lower molar on each side of its mouth. Because an elephant eats a lot of plants, its molars get ground down. New molars move in to replace the old molars about every ten years. An elephant gets up to six sets of molars over its lifetime.

Answer the following questions.

1. How many muscles and tendons are in an elephant's trunk?
   a. over 4,000 ( )
   b. over 40,000 ( )
   c. over 400,000 ( )
   d. over 40,000,000 ( )

2. What two things does an elephant use its trunk for?

= ______________________________

a. What are two things an elephant uses its tusks for?

= ______________________________

4. What does an elephant use its molars for?

a. growing tusks ( )
b. chewing plants ( )
c. chewing small animals ( )
d. speaking to another elephant ( )

Compare and Contrast Passages

Read the passage.

Two Fantastic Fruits

Bananas

Bananas are yellow fruits that grow in hot climates. They grow on tall plants in bunches called hands. They're easy to carry and fun to eat. Bananas are called the "perfect fruit" because they have many nutrients to keep you healthy. They have lots of potassium, which helps your muscles grow. For a delicious treat, add some banana slices to other foods, like cereal, ice cream, or a peanut butter sandwich. A banana is also an excellent breakfast food.

Pineapples

Pineapples are also yellow fruits that grow in hot climates. They grow on low plants close to the ground. Pineapples are very juicy and sweet. They are not easy to carry because they are big and have prickly skin. Pineapples are very healthy food. They have lots of vitamin C, which helps your body fight germs and helps build strong bones. Slices of pineapple taste wonderful when added to other foods, like pizza, ice cream, and hamburgers. Some people even put pineapple slices on cakes.

A. Tick the right option.

1. According to the paragraphs above, how are bananas and pineapples alike?
    a. They are both dirty fruits. ( )
    b. They both grow in bunches. ( )
    c. They are both easy to carry. ( )
    d. They both grow in hot climates. ( )

2. How are bananas and pineapples different?
    a. Pineapples are healthy, but bananas are not. ( )
    b. Bananas are easy to carry, but pineapples are not. ( )
    c. Pineapples grow on plants, but bananas do not. ( )
    d. Bananas and pineapples grow in hot climates. ( )

3. Which statement is an opinion?
    a. Some people put pineapple slices on cakes. ( )
    b. Bananas are a yellow fruit that grows in hot climates. ( )
    c. Pineapples have prickly skin. ( )
    d. Bananas taste delicious when added to cereal. ( )

B. What is a hand of bananas?

Ans: ____

21. Writing Skills or Composition

Picture Composition

Where a student observes a picture and tries to write some independent sentences against the picture.

Use Naming, Doing, and Describing words to form small sentences. Look at the example.

This is a picture of a garden.
There are many flowers in the garden.
A butterfly is near the flowers.
There is a big tree. A bird is sitting on it.

Write/Exercise

A. Look at the picture carefully, and write seven sentences about it.

1.
2.
3.

4.
5.
3.
7.

B. Look at the picture carefully, and try to point out things to write about them in simple sentences.

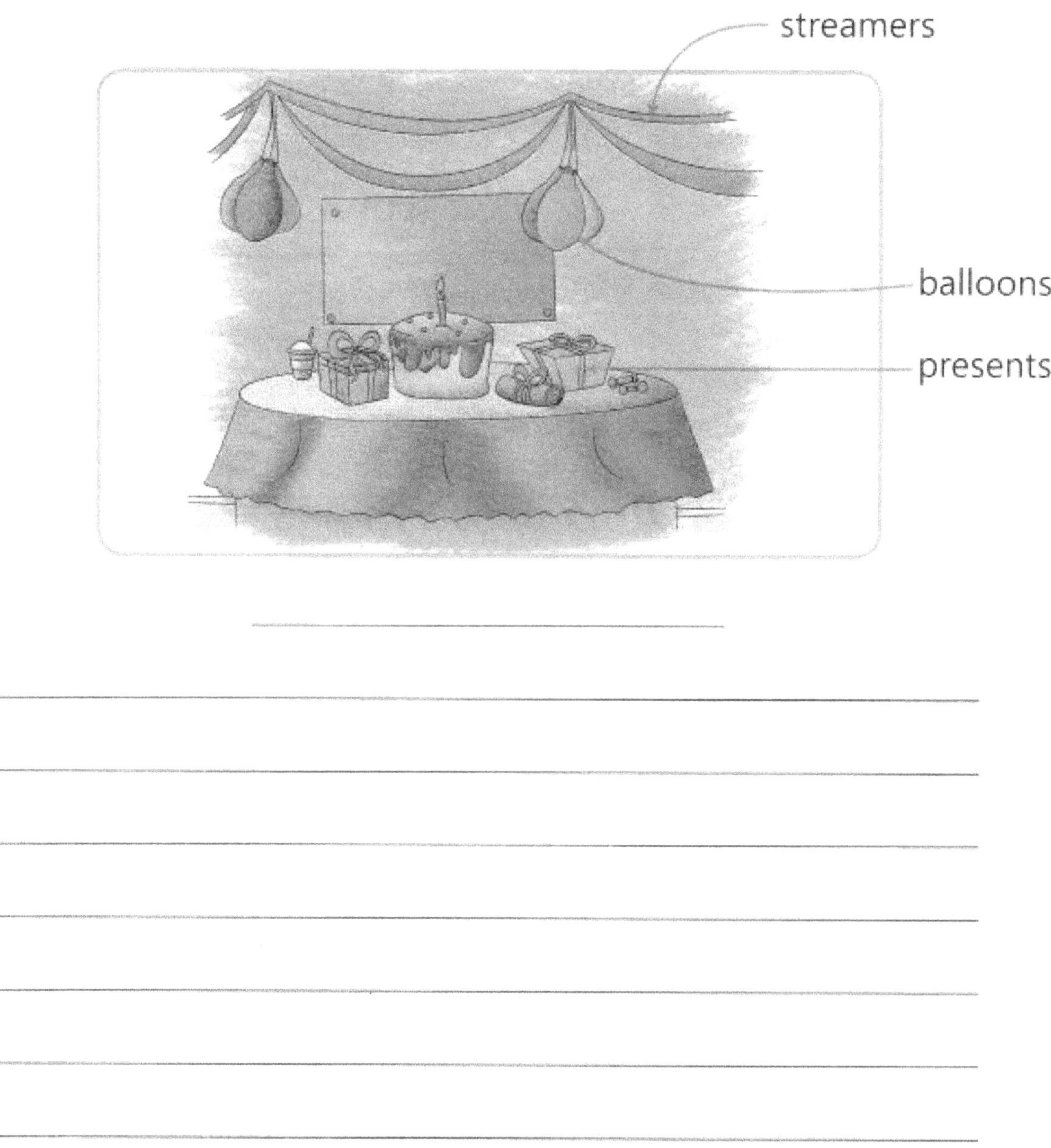

C. **Look at the following picture. Try to guess what this one is about. Write a few sentences on it:**

About Author

Mr. Sarkar, an esteemed educator from Bharat (formerly India) who authored the "New English Pal" series and many other academic and fictional works, has introduced A Common Guidebook of English Grammar and Composition for students of Primary Level. Additionally, Mr. Sarkar has authored other academic and fictional works available worldwide in eBook, Paperback, and Hardcover formats on platforms like Amazon, notionpress.com, Flipkart, Amazon Kindle, Google Play, and Google Books. The author extends his heartfelt appreciation to Amazon, notionpress.com, and Google for their invaluable support in publishing and marketing his works.

To locate his works, one can type the author's name or book title in the search box of any web browsers and platforms mentioned.

Thank you—happy reading.

Some important works by the writer & Co-author:

1. Study of Nouns, Pronouns, Adjectives & Articles (detail study) ISBN: 979-832-697-263-7 / 979-832-697-510-2
2. All about Verbs (Forms, Functions, Conjugation, Tense, Voice Change, Forming Questions & Negation) ISBN: 979-832-807-531-2 / 979-832-807-688-3
3. Study of Adverbs, Prepositions, Conjunctions & Interjections ISBN: 979-832-886-943-0 / 979-883-987-196-0
4. Detail Study of Phrases, Clauses & Sentences, including Idioms & Phrasal Verbs ISBN: 979-832-939-104-6 / 979-884-011-097-3
5. Study of Subject-Verb Agreement, Narration Change, and Use of Punctuation, including Analysis, Synthesis, & Split-up (Study through charts, division, explanation, and examples) ISBN: 979-880-723-013-3 / 979-888-704-674-7
6. **Peter's 'English Grammar, A Complete Version of English Grammar,** (detail study, explanation & examples)ISBN: 979-879-725-020-3 / 979-888-704-463-7
7. **Question Bank of English Grammar & Composition** (Learn through Exercises) ISBN: 979-883-531-890-2 / 979-888-733-132-4
8. **Rhetoric & Prosody** (A handbook of Figures of Speech, rhymes, feet of poetic lines for High School Students) ISBN: 979-840-526-645-9 / 979-888-684-952-3
9. **A Book of Advanced Writing Skill, the Complete Version** (incl Part-1, 2 & 3) ISBN: 979-836-472-826-5 / 979-888-869-835-8
10. **English *Grammar* & Question Bank Together** For Class VI to XII (Learn through Exercise) ISBN 979-838-571-382-0
11. **New English Pal,** Class **10** (A Complete Guide Book for Smart Learning, based on WBBSE syllabus) by **P. Sarkar, based on Peter's Grammar and Composition**: [Separate book for each class from 5 to 10]
12. **The Rainbow** (A Collection of Short Stories) ISBN 10: 979-832141310-4; 979-832141545-0 & ISBN 13: 979-889363024-4

Author page URL's:

https://www.amazon.com/author/mr.peter

https://www.amazon.in/~/e/B09QW2P4TY (Bharat/India)

https://www.amazon.co.uk/~/e/B09QW2P4TY

https://www.amazon.de/~/e/B09QW2P4TY

https://www.amazon.fr/~/e/B09QW2P4TY

https://www.amazon.co.jp/~/e/B09QW2P4TY

https://www.amazon.es/~/e/B09QW2P4TY

https://www.amazon.it/~/e/B09QW2P4TY

https://www.amazon.com.br/kindle-dbs/entity/author?asin=B09QW2P4TY

To locate his works, one can search by the book title or author's name on the web browsers and platforms mentioned. One may also use these links:

https://www.facebook.com/groups/mr.peter

https://notionpress.com/store/s?NP_Books%5Bquery%5D=Mr.+Peter

https://notionpress.com/store/s?NP_Books%5Bquery%5D=P.+Sarkar

The Following Coupons can be applied for discounts on **notionpress.com** till the end of the offers:

Coupon Codes	**Book Name**	**Buy for**	**Discount %**	**Rebate Prices**
Bulk13	Study of Nouns, Pronouns, Adjectives & Articles (detail study)	2 & more	52	~~300~~ 144
Bulk14	All about Verbs (Forms, Functions, Conjugation, Tense, Voice Change, Forming Questions & Negation)	2 & more	50	~~420~~ 210
~~PujaDeal3 / Deal3~~	Study of Adverbs, Prepositions, Conjunctions & Interjections	1 & more	~~20 & 26~~	290
Bulk15	Detail Study of Phrases, Clauses & Sentences, including Idioms & Phrasal Verbs	2 & more	52	~~290~~ 136
~~PujaDeal5 / Deal5~~	Study of Subject-Verb Agreement, Narration Change, Use of Punctuation; including Analysis, Synthesis & Split-up	1 & more	~~20 & 26~~	310
PujaDeal6 / Deal7	Question Bank of English Grammar & Composition	1 & more	20 & 28	~~559~~ 448 & 403
PujaDeal7 / Deal8/ bulk11	Rhetoric & Prosody	1 & more	20, 26 & 55	~~240~~ 192, 178 &108
~~PujaDeal8 / Deal9~~	Steps to Composition (Development of Writing Skill, from Primary to Secondary Level, Part-1)	~~1 & more~~	~~20 & 26~~	315
PujaDeal9 / Deal10	Development of Writing Skill, Part-2	1 & more	18 & 24	~~365~~ 300 & 278
PujaDeal10 / Deal11	Development of Writing Skill, Part-3	1 & more	18 & 24	~~365~~ 300 & 278
unique00 / bulk00	A Book of Advanced Writing Skill, the Complete Version (incl. Part-1, 2 & 3)	1 & more	15 & 23	~~780~~ 663 & 601
unique01 / bulk1/bulk10	Peter's 'English Grammar' (Complete Version of English Grammar)	1 & more	23, 30 & 48	~~1201~~ 925, 841 & 625
unique02/bulk02	English Grammar & Question Bank Together	1 & more	30 & 48	~~690~~ 483 & 359
spl01 / bulk04	New English Pal, Class 9 (based on WBBSE syllabus)	1 & more	35 & 47	~~490~~ 319 & 260
spl02 / bulk05	New English Pal, Class 10 (based on WBBSE syllabus)	1 & more	34 & 47	~~480~~ 317 & 255
spl03 / bulk06	New English Pal, Class 5 (based on WBBSE syllabus)	1 & more	29 & 52	~~280~~ 199 & 134
spl04 / bulk07	New English Pal, Class 8 (based on WBBSE syllabus)	1 & more	30 & 46	~~420~~ 294 & 227
spl05 / bulk08	New English Pal, Class 7 (based on WBBSE syllabus)	1 & more	30 & 54	~~400~~ 280 & 184
spl06 / bulk09	New English Pal, Class 6 (based on WBBSE syllabus)	1 & more	30 & 56	~~320~~ 224 & 141
spl07 / bulk12	The Rainbow (A Collection of Short Stories)	1 & more	56 & 56	~~299~~ 132 & 132
Note: For Copies of More Than One, Select The 2nd Coupon Given In Each Row of The First Column				

www.ingramcontent.com/pod-product-compliance
Lightning Source LLC
LaVergne TN
LVHW070229170826
845679LV00035B/1877
9798896100737